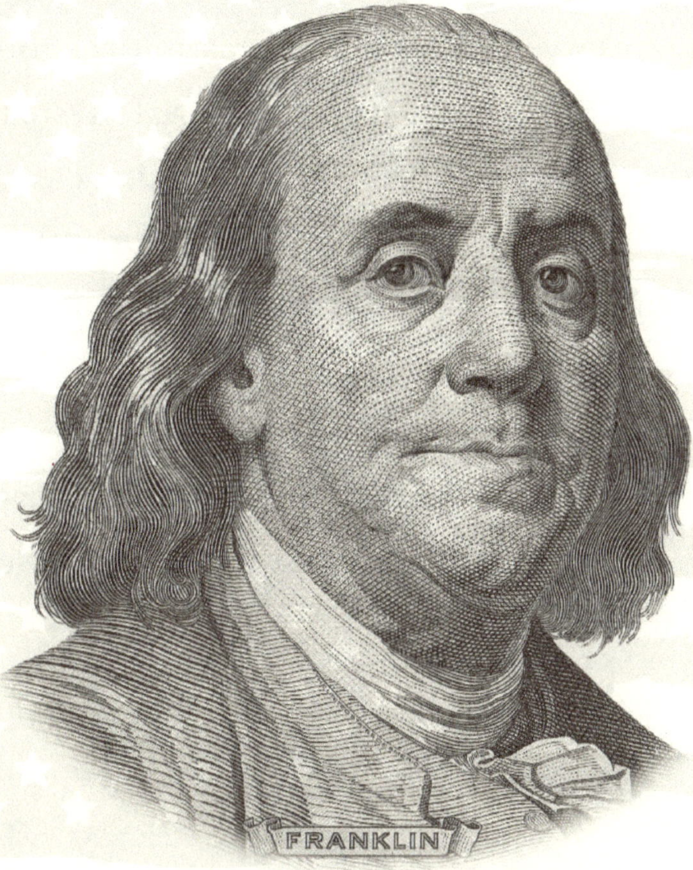

Benjamin Franklin

Biography for Teens

Copyright © KinZang 2022

All rights reserved. No part of this publication may be reproduced, stored in a retrieval system, or transmitted in any form or by any means, electronic, mechanical, photocopying, recording or otherwise, without either the prior written permissions of the author or publisher. This book may not be lent, resold, hired out or otherwise disposed of by way of trade in any form of binding or cover other than that in which it is published, without the prior consent of the author or publisher.

Acknowledgement
Free and paid images from www.Canva.com and Library of Congress.

CONTENTS

i.   *Introduction*   iii

I.   The Child   1

II.   The The Apprentice Printer   9

III. The Runaway   19

IV.   The Apprentice to Human
      Nature   23

V.   The Printer   35

VI.   The Community Builder   41

VII. The Moral Man   49

VIII. The Inventor   59

IX.   The Founding Father   69

X.   Wise Words   77

A publisher. A writer. An inventor. A statesman. A founding father of the United States of America. These words describe but only a part of one of the most illustrious American lives. Benjamin Franklin was indeed a man like no one during his times, perhaps that one person who defined the character of an entire nation.

Above everything he achieved in his life, Benjamin Franklin's life was ultimately a proof that the best life is the one that is self-made. He was born to crowded room full of competing siblings to a father who had picked up the trade of candle making. With many mouths to feed, food was never abundant but he learnt early on that industry and frugality are the antidotes for poverty.

Benjamin Franklin did not have much formal education: his father could afford a total of two full years of schooling for the young Franklin. But among his peers, he grew up to be one of the best minds America ever produced. From learning to speak multiple languages to mastering the human nature to conquering methods for uncovering scientific secrets, Benjamin Franklin learnt everything through, mostly, his love for books. In an era where books were rare and expensive, Benjamin was the biggest proponent of reading because his life exemplified the power of reading books.

But is Benjamin Franklin even relevant to us, two and a half centuries after his death? The answer is a resounding Yes!

Benjamin Franklin is not just a national hero. He was a man trying every day to become a better person for its own sake as well as for the service of his craft and his community that became a new nation. The mindset and the methods he used for his and his community's betterment is well-documented. And this is what makes him a historical figure whose life can still shine light on our lives.

I: The Child

Benjamin Franklin was born on 6 January 1706 in Boston. At the time of his birth, the United States of America did not exist as a country. Boston was a part of the Massachusetts Bay Colony. Boston's population of seven thousand people were mostly settlers who had come from England and other parts of Europe. Benjamin's father,

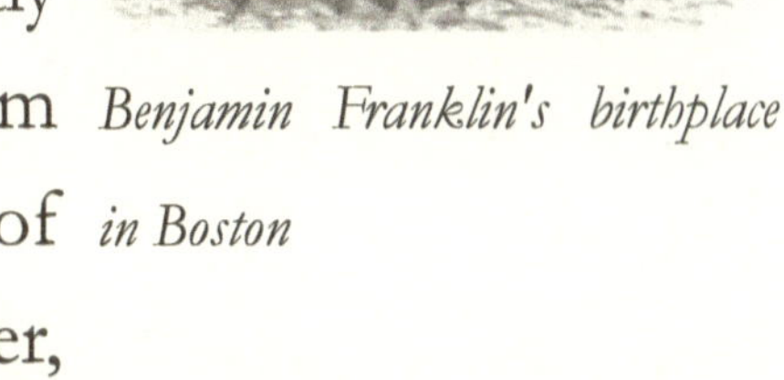

Benjamin Franklin's birthplace in Boston

Josiah Franklin, was also a settler who moved from England in 1683.

Benjamin's family was poor. His father supported the family by earning as a tallow chandler. A tallow chandler was someone who made candles from tallow, a form of animal fat. In those days, people used candles made from tallow to light their homes. His father's income could afford to rent only a tiny two-storied house in a place called Milk Street in Boston. Benjamin shared the house with his eleven brothers and sisters, and his two parents.

At the time of Benjamin's birth in 1706, Boston's total population was less than 9,000 people.

Benjamin's mother was Abiah Folger. His parents married in 1689 after his father's first wife died that year. In total, his father had seventeen children from two wives. That was a lot of children but those days that number of children was not unusual. Benjamin Franklin was the fifteenth child and the youngest son in the family.

Benjamin's father wanted him to become a clergyman. When Benjamin turned 8, he was sent to Boston Latin School which would also prepare him for college. In his first year in school, Benjamin excelled. In a short duration, he rose to the top of the class and was promoted by a grade in the same year.

However, Benjamin's character was not suitable for clergy. He was curious, skeptical and showed little respect for authority. Rather than listen to others, he liked asking questions and discovering things for himself. And he did not like saying long graces before meals. His father, realizing that Benjamin was unsuitable to become a clergyman, took him out of the Boston Latin School after one year and enrolled him in a writing and arithmetic academy. Some say he was taken out of Boston Latin School because his father could not afford. In the academy, Benjamin excelled in writing but failed in arithmetic. After one year, his father took him out of school and gave him a full-time job making candles. Benjamin was 10 years old.

Benjamin Franklin, who would later become writer, publisher, diplomat, inventor, philosopher and one of the founding fathers of the United States, had a total of two years of schooling in his entire life. He did not allow his lack of schooling to stop him from becoming one of the most knowledgeable persons of his time.

However, Benjamin hated his job as candle maker. And there was nothing much to like about it because it was not a pleasant work. Young Benjamin had to skim tallow from boiling pots of animal fat which smelt horrible. Cutting candle wicks and filling molds with tallow was mindless and extremely boring. Benjamin complained about the job and told his father he wanted to be a seaman.

Benjamin liked sea having born and lived near water. He had learnt early on to swim and manage boats and canoes.

However, one of Benjamin's brother had recently died at sea and Benjamin's father did not want to lose another son to the sea. Afraid that Benjamin might follow his dead brother, his father took him on long walks around Boston to see other craftsmen hoping Benjamin will find a job he liked on land.

On these long walks around Boston, Benjamin saw all sorts of craftsmen. He came across cutlers, bricklayers, wood turners, joiners and many more people working with different tools. Seeing these craftsmen at work left a lifelong impression on Benjamin. It spurred in him a deep interest to learn and work with tools with perfection.

Seeing Benjamin's interest, his father decided that it would be best for him to become a cutler, someone who made knives, scissors and other sharp instruments from metal.

In those days, people learnt a craft through apprenticeship. A young person would work as an apprentice under a master craftsman for many years until the apprentice learnt everything about the craft and became a craftsman. The only way for Benjamin to become a cutler was through years of apprenticeship.

So, Benjamin's father asked a close relative who was a cutler to take Benjamin as an apprentice. However, the relative demanded a fee rather than train Benjamin for free. Benjamin's father did not like this. Maybe he did not have money to pay. Unable to find free apprenticeship under a cutler for Benjamin, his father decided to make him an apprentice to one of his elder brothers called James who was a printer. Benjamin was 12 years at the time.

From a very young age, Benjamin was fond of reading books. Whenever he got little money, he would spend it on buying books. With his love for books and reading, Benjamin's father thought the printing apprenticeship was far more suitable for Benjamin. He now had access to plenty of reading materials and books. He made friends with people who had libraries and they lent him books.

In addition to reading, Benjamin loved writing. Whenever he got free time, he was either reading or writing, each day getting more knowledgeable and better at writing. Benjamin stayed as an apprentice to his brother till the age of 17.

II: The Apprentice Printer

When he was 12 years old, Benjamin Franklin was made an apprentice to his printer brother. As part of the agreement for apprenticeship, Benjamin could not drink or get married. He did not get paid but the agreement required his brother to provide him food, clothes and lodging while also teaching Benjamin the printing trade.

In those days, printing was a complicated task. First, the type was set. A type is a piece of metal with a letter, a number or a punctuation mark. To set the type, these letters, numbers and punctuation marks had to be arranged as the printer would like the final printed page to come. Type setting was a cumbersome task which took up to 25 hours of work to arrange the type to print one page of newspaper. Once the type was set, ink was applied on the type which was then pressed on the paper to get a printed page.

As an apprentice, Benjamin's job involved washing, sorting and setting type. He also had to work the press. Every Thursday, he delivered newspaper that came out the printing press he worked.

A printer working a printing press

But Benjamin had insatiable desire for learning. For that, he did not need school. Working as an apprentice printer brought Benjamin in touch with people who liked and owned books. Those days, good books were rare and expensive. Seeing his love for books, these people lent books to Benjamin and reading books spurred his interest in writing.

Benjamin's earliest writing works were two ballads. One was called The Lighthouse Tragedy. It was about a captain who drowned at sea along with his two daughters. The other was about the capture of a pirate called Blackbeard. He printed both the works and sold them in the town. People liked it which encouraged Benjamin to write more. However, his father told him that verse-makers were beggars. So, Benjamin gave up writing verse and instead put his effort into writing prose.

Benjamin used a number of strategies to write better. One involved exchanging letters. He had a friend with whom he liked to debate and argue. When they could not meet in person, they wrote letters to each other, making arguments and counterarguments on some issues.

The second way Benjamin built his writing skills was

by using other people's works. One day, Benjamin came across an old volume of a journal called The Spectator. It contained essays written by two writers called Joseph Addison and Richard Steele. This journal was published in London but an old copy found its way into the hands of Benjamin in Boston.

Benjamin liked the essays of *The Spectator* and he wanted to imitate them. He read them over and over again, taking careful notes of how the essays presented ideas and what emotions the sentences evoked. After a few days, he wrote the essays in his own words and compared his version with the originals. When he came across mistakes he had made, he corrected them. He would mix the thoughts and arguments in the essays and then after a few days try to arrange them. While his versions were not as good as the original essays, he felt in certain parts he had improved upon the original works. This encouraged Benjamin to imagine that he could actually become a good writer.

From thereon, Benjamin practiced writing at every opportunity. He read and wrote at night after work and in the morning before starting to work. On Sundays, instead of going to the church which his father expected, Benjamin pretended to be working at the printing house so that he can practice writing. When his brother and other workers took long lunch breaks, Benjamin was busy reading and doing writing exercises.

Benjamin also studied other subjects. During his second year of schooling, he failed in arithmetic and Benjamin was often shamed for his ignorance of numbers and figures. So, he also started reading books on numbers and navigation. But more than mathematics, he liked philosophy, rhetoric and logic. He was deeply impressed by Socratic method of argumentation which teaches the learner to make positive arguments through questions rather than through direct contradictions. Using this method, he could force even people with superior knowledge to concede defeat.

His biggest opportunity to show his writing skills came when his brother James started a newspaper called the New England Courant in 1721. This was the second newspaper in America and it was based on the English journal The Spectator in content and style. Benjamin had by then developed his self-taught style which was unique and liked by his readers. He wanted to write for his brother's newspaper. But it was never meant to be.

James was already jealous of Benjamin's growing popularity as a write protégé. He did not want Benjamin to outshine him as a writer. Therefore, despite Benjamin's repeated pleas to his brother to allow him to write for the newspaper, James refused to even let him talk about it. With his hunger for writing, Benjamin devised a clever trick to write for the newspaper.

One day, Benjamin wrote an essay using a pen name and a disguised handwriting. The character he used for the pseudonym was a widow from a rural area called Mrs. Silence Dogood. In this essay, Benjamin wrote an imaginary story about the life history of Mrs. Silence Dogood and how she came to live in Boston from England. At night, he slipped the essay under the door of his brother's printing house.

The next morning, James and his friends were excited to see a well-written anonymous essay in their hands. As James and friends marveled at the essay and decided to publish it, Benjamin chuckled silently at them. The essay came out on the frontpage of the newspaper.

Encouraged by this, Benjamin wrote a total of 14 essays under the pen name. The essays became popular among the readers of the New England Courant. His brother James encouraged Mrs. Silence Dogood to keep sending in more essays. Some men also wrote letters to the newspaper offering to marry Mrs. Silence Dogood.

Even though Benjamin was only 16 years when he wrote the 14 essays as Mrs. Silence Dogood, the essays were a literary masterpiece. It showed his creativity and the power of his imagination to see the world through the eyes of a much older widow. Most importantly, these essays paved way for American writers to build a unique American style of writing.

This period in Benjamin's life had profound influence on his later part of life. The writing skills he developed when he was an apprentice helped him become one of the best American writers. His knowledge in printing and working with machines enabled him to become a knowledgeable printer.

However, his apprenticeship with his brother was challenging. Rather than love him as a brother, James treated Benjamin with tyranny. He grew increasingly jealous of Benjamin's ability to learn fast and write well. When Benjamin revealed that he was indeed Mrs. Silence Dogood, James turned furious rather than be happy for his brother who helped make his newspaper popular. James was intent on stopping Benjamin from shining. Many times, he beat Benjamin for no reasons. When Benjamin threatened to leave his brother's printing house and work for other printer, James went to all the printers and told them what a terrible person Benjamin was in order to prevent him from finding work with any printers in Boston. The way his brother treated him made

Benjamin become a lifelong hater of arbitrary power.

Even more painful for young Benjamin was his father's support for James when they quarreled. Seeing no point in working for his brother or staying in Boston, Benjamin ran away.

III: The Runaway

It was a tradition among early American pioneers to pack up and go to the frontiers when the communities they lived in became too constricting. For Benjamin Franklin, Boston was becoming increasingly cramped for his free, pioneering spirit. His mockery of religion has made him many enemies in Boston and the lies his brother spread about him meant he could not find any printer in Boston to employ him. On the other hand, the abuse he suffered at the hands of his brother had become unbearable. He had to leave Boston.

On September 25, 1723, the 17-year old Benjamin fled Boston for New York. He did not tell his parents that he was leaving Boston. He was afraid they would try to stop him. He sold some of his books to raise some money and bought a one-way boat ticket for New York. He arrived in New York three days later, with no knowledge of anyone and little money.

Having worked in his brother's printing house in Boston, he offered to work for a printer in New York called William Bradford. The printer had no job for Benjamin in New York but told him to go to Philadelphia. William's son had a printing house in Philadelphia and was in need of a worker after the previous worker died. Benjamin decided to go to Philadelphia, another 100 miles away from New York.

However, the journey from New York to Philadelphia proved to be a challenging one for Benjamin. The boat he took got stranded in the water and he and other passengers nearly died of thirst.

After reaching ashore, he got ill but got up and walked for a full day in rain to reach the ferry that would talk him to Philadelphia. But he was late for the regular ferry and he had to hitch a ride in a boat which they had to row till the destination. Despite the hardship he faced on the way, never did he think once of turning back and returning to Boston. It was never an option.

Benjamin arrived in Philadelphia on October 6, 1723, exhausted and hungry, wearing dirty and torn clothes and little money. He indeed did make quite an opening in Philadelphia. He was worried he might be thought of a runaway and captured. In his own words:

I was dirty from my journey; my pockets were stuff'd out with shirts and stockings, and I knew no soul nor where to look for lodging. I was fatigued with travelling, rowing, and want of rest, I was very hungry; and my whole stock of cash consisted of a Dutch dollar, and about a shilling in copper.

The first business for him after arrival was to buy himself some food. For three pennies he could spare, he was given three rolls of bread. With a bread roll each under his arms while munching on the third, he wandered the Market Street of Philadelphia. He made such an unusual and ridiculous spectacle that it even caught the eyes of a woman who would later become his wife. And this was how one of the most important residents of Philadelphia made his start: as a hungry, poor young man.

Benjamin Franklin arriving in Philadelphia as a runaway

IV: The Apprentice To Human Nature

In Philadelphia, Benjamin Franklin found a job at a printing house owned by a person called Samuel Keimer. But this phase of Benjamin's life was important not for his printing job but the knowledge he gained about human nature. The understanding of humans he developed during this period would prov to be the key to his rise as a successful and respectable public figure later on.

Observe Other People with a Sharp Eye

When we are taken out of our familiar settings and put in a new, unfamiliar place with no one that we can turn to, we learn to be more observant. This can be a matter of our survival. Arriving in Philadelphia with nothing more than stained clothes on his back, Benjamin had to develop a sharp eye and a keen ear for other people.

His first lesson came from his new employer Keimer. Benjamin was introduced to Keimer by William Bradford, the printer who Benjamin met in New York. Keimer, however, had not met William before and did not know that William's son also had a printing house, a competitor, in Philadelphia. Not knowing that he was talking to a competitor, Keimer bragged and revealed all his plans to capture printing business from his competitors while William made Keimer talk more and spill all his secrets by asking artful questions. Benjamin could see the difference between a crafty expert and a novice, and came away convinced that his new employer was not the sharpest tool in the shed.

Do Not Evoke Envy in Other People

It is best not to make other people envious of you; this can be harmful for you. Benjamin got a taste of this not long after he started working for Keimer. Benjamin's superior skills as a printer brought him to the attention of Philadelphia's governor, Sir William Keith. Benjamin became well-liked by the governor and the two dined together many times. This made Keimer deeply jealous of Benjamin. He would later try to make Benjamin pay for it.

Envy is a natural trait of most people. And envious people always make it difficult for people they envy. However, Benjamin was too naïve to see how other people's jealousy toward him was affecting him. He did not realize that his printer brother James treated him badly due to the envy he had evoked in his brother with his superior writing skills. And unwittingly, he made it worse.

This happened when Benjamin visited his home in Boston seven months after first landing in Philadelphia. Dressed in a shiny new suit and pockets stuffed with a watch and a lot of money, he visited his brother James at his printing house. Young men whom he had worked with at the printing house gathered around Benjamin to see his new clothes. They were simply awed by the stories of his friendship with the governor and the success he found in Philadelphia. He showed them his money in silver and his new watch. Before he left, he gave them some money for them to buy drinks. All these offended his brother James deeply. He went from jealousy to outright hatred for Benjamin and any chances of them coming to good terms as brothers were gone.

Many years later, Benjamin started a book sharing group in Philadelphia. As it grew in popularity, Benjamin observed that some people were becoming unhappy at him for getting all the attention. This could ruin the venture. To prevent this, he used his knowledge of people to keep the envious people happy. Instead of taking all the praises for himself, he put other people in the front while he took the backstage. When he had good ideas, he would give the credit to other people. They became more interested in supporting the ideas. Using this method,

Benjamin was able to keep the support of other people to continue with the venture.

Trust not the words but actions of other people

We can get easily carried away by other people's convincing words. But more than words, we should learn to observe their actions. We should trust their actions more than their words. Benjamin learnt this the hard way.

Benjamin Franklin was one of earliest known femenist. He supported women's education knowing that women are equally capable as men. And he was all praises for women doing businesses.

Sir William Keith, the governor of Philadelphia, liked Benjamin's skills as a printer. He showered Benjamin with praises and glowing promises that he would help Benjamin set up his own printing press. He urged Benjamin to travel to England to buy the printing press and bring it back to Philadelphia. To help Benjamin get the printing press in England, Sir William Keith promised to write to his friends in England to help Benjamin buy the press on credit.

With high hopes, Benjamin sailed to England, leaving behind his future wife. He had little money and only the promise of the governor.

Only after reaching England did he find out that the governor had lied. The governor had not sent any letters to his friends in England to issue credit to Benjamin. He found out that the governor was not in a position to help him at all and everyone who knew the governor had no trust in him at all. The governor was, after all, just a bag of wind. He was a con man. This left Benjamin once again in the streets, this time in London. It took him almost two years of working in London to afford to return to Philadelphia.

The long cross-Atlantic sea journey gave him enough time to reflect on what he needed to do to succeed among people. By the time he returned to Philadelphia, he had learnt his lessons well. And he put his learning to use immediately.

In Philadelphia, he was hired again by his former employer Keimer. Since Benjamin had now become more observant of other people, he could see there was something different about the way Keimer treated him. Keimer has always been grumpy and sullen around Benjamin before but now he has suddenly become cheerful. He even paid Benjamin much higher wages than before. These made Benjamin doubtful of Keimer's intentions and he went about finding out what Keimer really was up to. It did not take long for Benjamin to uncover Keimer's true intentions.

Benjamin found out that Keimer was not happy that Benjamin left his job with him and went to England. Since Benjamin was an experienced and a skillful printer, Keimer's business suffered after he left as there was no one who could replace Benjamin. For this, Keimer held a deep grudge against Benjamin. When Benjamin returned from England, all Keimer wanted Benjamin to do was teach his other workers. Once he was done milking Benjamin dry off his skills, Benjamin concluded that Keimer would no longer need him. Keimer would then fire Benjamin when he was least expecting, thus getting his revenge.

With this knowledge, Benjamin went about making his own plans. Instead of waiting for Keimer to fire him, Benjamin silently created his own printing business, building friendship with influential people and Keimer's important customers.

It turned out that Benjamin's assessment of Keimer's intentions was correct. Once Benjamin had trained other workers enough, Keimer started to become increasingly hostile toward him. But when Keimer knew his workers did not have the skills to do a particular job and when he had to depend on Benjamin, Keimer suddenly became friendly and generous to Benjamin. But once the job was done, he grew cold towards Benjamin again. Just when Keimer was about to throw out Benjamin from his job, Benjamin left Keimer. When he left, he took other skillful workers and important customers from Keimer with him. Benjamin's observation skills saved him from ruins.

Benjamin came away unharmed from Keimer's manipulation. Generally, we feel anger and hatred when we fall victim to manipulative people.

Benjamin, however, felt no anger or hatred toward Keimer. Instead, he felt elated that his observation of people proved correct. He felt enriched.

Learn to See the World through the eyes of Other People

When we are young, we think that our intelligence and charm can get us what we want from other people. We use our character to impress others and play on their emotions to get our way. Certainly, Benjamin worked his way through some of the challenges using his charm and knowledge. This approach to influence people works when the stakes are low. But in the real world, when stakes get high, this method is ineffective. We need to get to the next level. We need to understand other people's intentions. For this, we need to learn to see the world through the eyes of other people.

Benjamin had a knack for imagining the world from another person's point of view. When he wrote the 14 essays under the pen name Mrs. Silence Dogood, he convinced all the readers that the essays were in fact written by a woman because Benjamin put himself in the shoes of his character. But it was only when he was working at printing press in London did he truly appreciate the importance of the ability to imagine the world through the eyes of another person.

After Benjamin was sent to London under the false promise of governor William Keith, he had to work for a printing house to survive in the big city. In the printing house, there was a strange culture: everyone had to contribute a certain portion of their wages to a common fund from which workers bought and drank cheap beer. Benjamin, who did not drink alcohol, refused to pay. This was a mistake.

All of a sudden, errors started appearing in Benjamin's works, errors which Benjamin would otherwise never make. The moment Benjamin turned his back, someone would plant mistakes in his work. When he confronted the workers, they said it was perhaps the phantom, a ghost, who did the mischief. The only way for Benjamin to get out of this problem was to join the workers and be a part of their group. The moment he joined the group and paid the group membership fee, the deliberate errors in his works vanished.

Benjamin would never drink alcohol and as a professional it was unacceptable for him to show up at work with alcoholic breath. He would never go to such a level. But the only way for him to stay out of the harm's way and keep his job was to join those drunkards. He had to go down to their level and experience the world through their eyes. From this position, it even became easier for Benjamin to influence these people because he was no longer seen as an outsider.

In the age of technology and high ideas, it is easy for us to dismiss such skills in dealing with other people as unnecessary. We feel we can get our way by using only ideas, reasoning and persuasion to influence people. But influencing by this method has limits. What Benjamin has taught us is that the surest way for us to safeguard against other people's ill intentions toward us and influence them is through understanding other people at a deeper level. For Benjamin certainly, his knowledge of people was the master key that opened doors to a colorful life he led.

V: The Printer

After Benjamin left his job at Keimer's, he started his printing business. He was the third printer in Philadelphia, through a partnership with a friend. Like all things worth doing, starting his printing business did not come easy. Printing was a laborious job entailing long days. He had to find the capital to purchase the machines and a cheap house to rent. There was also competitions to beat. But it was his printing business that made Benjamin wealthy. Along the way, he learnt many lessons of life.

Lend no Ears to Prophets of Doom

We come across nay-sayers and prophets of doom everywhere. And they are the loudest when we are doing something new and exciting. Benjamin came across such a croaker soon after he set up his own printing business in Philadelphia. A man named Samuel Mickle came to meet Benjamin after learning of his new business. His only purpose was to tell Benjamin how sorry he was for Benjamin's expensive business which was doomed to fail since people in Philadelphia were already going bankrupt.

This man did plant a doubt in Benjamin's mind. The croaker was so persuasive in his assurance about Benjamin's business going bankrupt that Benjamin thought he would not have started his business if he had come across the man before he started his venture. Of course, for Benjamin, it was too late not to start because he had already started his business and there was no going back.

The biggest mistake we can make is to listen to such cynics. They do not know any better but they can see only failure and doom in everything. Benjamin was later pleased to see the croaker buy a house paying five times as much as he would have paid had he been not such a cynic and bought it earlier.

Show Your Work

Competing with two established printers was not easy. But Benjamin's determination to make his business succeed and his hard work did not go unnoticed. When he had a job to finish, he would be the last person to go to bed and the first one to rise to get the job done. When people, especially people who shape opinions, noticed his effort and skills, good words about his printing business spread and his business thrived.

Hard work, industry as Benjamin called, was a lifelong characteristic of Benjamin. He learnt the value of hard work from his father. He recalled:

I from thence considered industry as a means of obtaining wealth and distinction, which encourag'd me, tho' I did not think that I should ever literally stand before kings, which, however, has since happened; for I have stood before five, and even had the honor of sitting down with one, the King of Denmark, to dinner.

One such profitable business was printing paper money. When Philadelphia needed more paper money to be printed, Benjamin got the job through his skills and dedication, and the respect he had of the legislators. It is no wonder that the US hundred-dollar bill still carries his smile.

Guard Your Secrets

Soon after he started his printing business, Benjamin saw profit in starting a newspaper. The only newspaper in Philadelphia called The American Weekly Mercury had extremely boring contents but it still made profit for its owner. Benjamin was confident that his entertaining and engaging writings would attract readers and therefore profit. But he made a mistake of telling his intent to another person, who happened to be a loudmouth. He did not keep the secret and instead told Keimer who immediately started printing a newspaper in 1728.

Of course, Keimer who lacked any good taste and linguistic flair named his newspaper The Universal

Instructor in all Arts and Sciences: and Pennsylvania Gazette. Its content was equally dull. Barely a year later, Keimer put up the newspaper for sale. Benjamin partnered with a friend to buy it and renamed it as The Pennsylvania Gazette. Over the ensuing years, the newspaper became the most popular one among the colonies.

Gradually, Benjamin's printing business started bringing him a steady income. His profit also came from his stationary shop. Despite his steady income, Benjamin remained frugal in his spending. He dressed plainly, he did not drink or spend time in ideal diversion, and he never wasted time going fishing or shooting. His industry and frugal living enhanced his social standing which brought him respect and business.

At the same time, his former employer Keimer's business declined daily until he was forced to sell off his business and run away to Barbadoes Island where he died a poor man.

In 1730, Benjamin married Deborah Read, who first

saw Benjamin in October 1723 holding two bread rolls under his arm while munching on another, in poor clothes and wandering the street of Philadelphia.

VI: The Community Builder

As Benjamin became more established financially in Philadelphia, he diverted his attention to improving the conditions of his fellow countrymen. Onte by one, he put his ideas into action, all the while driven solely by his desire to make his community more vibrant. The following list is but only a few of Benjamin's vast contribution to his society that had lasting impact.

The Junto

In 1727, at the age of 21, Benjamin founded a group called Junto, from the Spanish word junta meaning assembly. The Junto consisted of twelve members who came from diverse occupations and they were printers, surveyors, a cabinetmaker, a shoemaker, a clerk and a bartender. The members shared one common interest: a spirit of enquiry and a desire to improve themselves and their community. The members met every Friday to discuss issues of importance to themselves and the community. Benjamin was only 21 years old when he started Junto. While the other members were clearly older than him, Benjamin was their leader.

Benjamin later proposed that the members start a common library. Members would bring their books and exchange with books of others. Books were expensive then but pooling the books, it was the same as every member owning the entire library. It was another example of Benjamin's self-learning and self-improvement initiatives for the betterment of himself as well as the community.

The group did make a start in book sharing but bringing books from home and exchanging it was cumbersome. The idea failed and the books went back to their respective owners. However, this failure led to a bigger and a highly successful initiative whose presence continue to the day.

Subscription Library

In 1731, the Junto members started the first ever subscription library. During that time, buying books in Philadelphia was prohibitively expensive. The books had to be purchased either from New York or Boston. Only the wealthy could afford to buy. To make books accessible to the general public, the Junto members combined their books and kept them in a meeting room from where subscribers could borrow, the first subscription library. It was called the Library Company of Philadelphia.

There were fifty subscribers initially. The subscribers paid a fixed amount to purchase new books and another amount as annual fee. Over time, the subscribers increased. The Library Company ordered books from England on a wide range of subjects. As donations and new purchases increased, the library had to be moved to bigger locations. The subscription library, which popped up throughout the colonies, had a huge impact on the education in the colonies. In his autobiography, Benjamin wrote:

These libraries have improved the general conversation of the Americans, made the common tradesmen and farmers as intelligent as most gentlemen from other countries, and perhaps have contributed in some degree to the stand so generally made throughout the colonies in defense of their privileges.

At the same time, the flourishing library had its own benefit for Benjamin. He wrote:

This library afforded me the means of improvement by constant study, for which I set apart an hour or two each day, and thus repaired in some degree the loss of the learned education my father once intended for me. Reading was the only amusement I allowed myself. I spent no time in taverns, games, or frolicks of any kind; and my industry in my business continued as indefatigable as it was necessary.

Fire and Insurance Company

In 1730, Benjamin took up the cause of fire safety following a series of fire accidents. A particular incident left a deep impression on him. That year, a fire started on a ship and burnt the wharf and three nearby houses. Benjamin wrote a paper for his group, Junto, proposing for the need of forming a company to extinguish fires and provide help in saving properties.

The first fire brigade was formed by 26 volunteers. Each volunteer brought six buckets to carry water and two bags to salvage properties. Volunteers organized themselves into groups managing water, protecting properties, training and fire prevention. More volunteers signed up and the fire company became equipped with fire engines and ladders. The results were immediately visible. When other towns lost entire blocks to fire accidents, Philadelphia's losses were one or two houses at a time. The Philadelphia Fire Company of today traces its roots to Benjamin's fire company which was a model for other fire company across the United States.

Another contribution of Benjamin to his community was the fire insurance company. He created the Philadelphia Contributionship for the Insurance of Houses from Loss of Fire. It offered polices to cover the cost of damage caused to homes by fires. Today it exists as Philadelphia Contributionship, which is the oldest successful property insurance company in the United States.

Defense

In 1739, the War of Jenkins's Ear broke out between Great Britain and Spain. Eight years earlier, sailors of the Spanish coast guard boarded a British merchant ship in the Caribbean captained by one Robert Jenkins as a part of routine search for contraband. During the course of the search, the Spanish sailors cut off Jenkins's ear. The earless captain was used by the British parliament to call for war with Spain, thus the name of the war.

As the war between two European heavyweights raged, France joined the war and threw its weight behind Spain. English colonies were in real danger from the Spanish and French forces. In Philadelphia, the effort by the Governor to pass a militia law did not succeed. Given the defenseless situation, Benjamin proposed for a voluntary militia. This proved to be a huge success as hundreds of men signed up on the first day. It then grew to ten thousand strong force. The men organized themselves into their own companies and regiments with commanding officers while women did their own part to support the militia.

Benjamin was offered the position of Colonel for his role in starting the association. But he declined the offer since he had no military experience. Instead he took the role of a common soldier.

The University of Philadelphia

In 1749, Benjamin presented a vision for education through a pamphlet titled "Proposals Relating to the Education of Youth of Pennsylvania". This led to the opening of an academy that later became the present-day University of Pennsylvania.

VII: The Moral Man

One of the reasons Benjamin Franklin remains a favorite historical figure two and a half centuries after his death is that he left behind plenty of things for us to learn from his illustrious life. Take, for instance, his lifelong pursuit of self-improvement.

t

Soon after he started his printing business in Philadelphia, he decided on a bold objective: to achieve moral perfection. Like most people in his day, Benjamin was religious. But the path shown by the church was inadequate. Benjamin did not quite like the church's insistence on rituals while neglecting completely a person's moral development. When he found this gap, Benjamin decided to ditch the church on Sundays and instead go on his own path to achieve moral perfection.

Benjamin's wish was to live without committing any fault at any time. He would conquer all bad habits and do the right thing every time. This was, of course, easier said than done. He would find himself slipping back into old habits. When he guarded against one fault, another fault would creep in. He decided that overcoming bad habits was not enough, that it needed to be replaced with good ones.

Using his wide knowledge from reading books, he drew up a list of thirteen virtues he committed to live by at all times to become a morally perfect person. In his own words, the thirteen virtues were:

1. TEMPERANCE. Eat not to dullness; drink not to elevation.

2. SILENCE. Speak not but what may benefit others or your- self; avoid trifling conversation.

3. ORDER. Let all your things have their places; let each part of your business have its time.

4. RESOLUTION. Resolve to perform what you ought; per- form without fail what you resolve.

5. FRUGALITY. Make no expense but to do good to others or yourself; i.e., waste nothing.

6. INDUSTRY. Lose no time; be always employed in some- thing useful; cut off all unnecessary actions.

7. SINCERITY. Use no hurtful deceit; think innocently and justly, and, if you speak, speak accordingly.

8. JUSTICE. Wrong none by doing injuries, or omitting the benefits that are your duty.

9. MODERATION. Avoid extremes; forbear resenting injuries so much as you think they deserve.

10. CLEANLINESS. Tolerate no uncleanliness in body, clothes, or habitation.

11. TRANQUILLITY. Be not disturbed at trifles, or at accidents common or unavoidable.

12. CHASTITY. Rarely use venery but for health or offspring, never to dullness, weakness, or the injury of your own or another's peace or reputation.

13. HUMILITY. Imitate Jesus and Socrates.

For Benjamin, it was not enough to settle on a list of virtues. His goal was to make them a habit, a part of him. To turn those qualities into habit, he devised an effective method to measure and keep track of his progress. Even then he knew instinctively that what you can't measure, you can't improve. At the center of this method was a one-page journal:

	Sun	Mon	Tue	Wed	Thu	Fri	Sat
T.	**	*					
S							
O			*				
R							
F	**		*				
I							
S		*		**			
J							
M							
C							
T							
C							
H							

The letters on the first column were the initials of the thirteen virtues Benjamin was trying to develop.

Benjamin knew that attempting to improve on all his virtues at the same time would be a mistake. Instead, he decided to take on one virtue at a time. For one full week, every day, he would work on improving only one virtue. In thirteen weeks, he would complete one round and in one year, 52 weeks, he would complete four rounds.

The way he measured his progress was simple. Every evening, Benjamin would go through his day to review if he lived the day according to the virtue he was trying to develop that day. For instance, Benjamin worked on improving the quality of temperance during the first week. When he reviewed his words and actions of the day in the evening, and if, for example, he indulged in eating excessively for lunch, he would mark with a black spot. Every black spot in the journal was a mistake of words or actions that was not in keeping with the virtue he was trying to develop. In the following days, he would try to remove all the black spots from his journal, to make the page free of any black spots of his bad habits. By living in words and actions according to his virtues, his journal page became cleaner, with the black spots growing fewer over time.

One of the biggest mistakes in life is that we pull brakes on self-improvement early on life. We stop learning the moment we get out of school. We do not pursue new skills once we get a job and we struggle through life with the burdens of our imperfections and limitations, when it would be far easier if we keep up the habit of self-improvement. More than before, we need to work on self-improvement.

Our aversion to self-development is mostly cultural. In our culture, the idea that someone is either born good or bad at something is very powerful. For example, a child is naturally good or bad at math or science. This idea is powerful but false. Nature gives only potential. Whether a child is good or bad at math depends entirely on how much effort the child puts into learning math. No one has more or less natural talent. Effort is what separates the good from the bad.

Benjamin, who had only two years of schooling in his entire life, proved that a person can become educated without schooling and can become successful in life through effort and dedication. He showed that what is required is the personal initiative.

The method Benjamin worked out to develop moral perfection is a powerful tool that you need to adopt to bring lasting change in life. The reason is simple: success is not something you find; success is something you attract by the person you become.

At the most basic level, what separates a successful person from a failure is that a successful person has qualities, or virtues as Benjamin called, of success while a failure has qualities of failure. Certain qualities attract success while others repeal success. For instance, to be economically successful, we need to have qualities such as hard work, intelligence and determination. Without these qualities in you, it will be difficult to attract success. To become successful, we need to build the qualities that attract success, and eliminate qualities that repeal success.

Here is how you can use Benjamin's method in your own life. Study successful people you admire. Study not their life or words, but the qualities and virtues they possess. If Steve Jobs, the founder of Apple, is a person you admire, study the qualities he had that made him a visionary. If you want to become a successful writer, study famous writers. Understand their dominant habits and qualities that led them on a path to success. Once you identify the habits and qualities, use Benjamin's method to make those habits a part of you. This is indeed how lasting transformation is achieved.

Another reason why this method works is that it measures your actions. When it comes to results, thoughts and intentions count for little. We can have brilliant ideas but if we do not have the discipline to translate them into actions, ideas remain as ideas. Only words and actions matter. Ideas are cheap; actions are what counts. If your actions do not reflect your virtues, it does not matter what thoughts you hold. That is why, use your words and actions as measures for the qualities you are trying to develop.

It takes an honest look at our actions to understand how they affect us. That is the only way we can change ourselves. At first, Benjamin was surprised to find so many faults and black spots in his daily conduct. You will also find, if you are honest enough, that you are full of faults. Finding faults and problems takes you half way to solving them. Like Benjamin, when you work on your faults, you correct them.

VIII: The Inventor

Benjamin was a curious child, always observant of people and things around him, and never shying away from experimenting. Everything was interesting to him and he was always on the lookout to understand better and make things better. His insatiable curiosity led him on an invention spree and scientific discovery which brought him much admiration and respect from the scientific community, most notably, in Europe. Some of Benjamin's inventions continue to be used today, a proof of how far ahead his inventions really were.

Swimming Pads

One of the earliest inventions of Benjamin was the swimming pads. Benjamin had learnt swimming from an early age. When he was eleven years old, he invented the swimming pads. It was made of wood, in oval shape, measuring 10 inches by six inches with a hole each for the two thumbs. They resembled the painter's pallets. With the help of these pads, he was able to swim much faster. But the pads fatigued his wrists and he gave up using them. Much later in 1933, a Frenchman by the name Louis de Corlieu reinvented the pads, which was much similar in concept to Benjamin's.

Even before that, Benjamin awed his gang of boys by using a kite to drag him over the water. By holding the string of a flying kite, he would float away effortlessly, dragged by the kite. Benjamin also tried swim fins for his legs, but they did not work.

Benjamin was a big proponent of swimming as a

great physical exercise. This was itself revolutionary at a time when physical comfort was highly sought after. During his time in London, he was fond of swimming across Thames. One time, on a boat ride, he impressed other passengers by jumping into the sea and swimming alongside the boat. Benjamin's early advocacy of swimming has earned him a spot in the International Swimming Hall of Fame and the United States Swim School Association Hall of Fame.

Franklin Stove

In 1742, Benjamin revolutionized home heating. In his day, colonists in Pennsylvania staved off the frigid winters by burning logs in their fireplaces. These were highly inefficient, burning a lot of wood while most of the heat escaped through the chimney. Every now and then, sparks from the roaring fireplaces escaped and ignited the house on fire. A few decades in, the colonists cleared the forest around Philadelphia and they had to travel much farther away to collect wood. To resolve this early energy crisis, Franklin invented the Franklin Stove.

Franklin Stove was made up of a cast-iron box. It radiated heat from all sides and the heat was controlled by adjusting the airflow and the burn rate. It was safe and highly efficient in terms of fuel consumption and heat generation. The stoves used today in log cabins around the world are more or less the same as the one Benjamin invented.

Glass Armonica

In 1750s, while living in England as a Pennsylvania diplomat, Benjamin stopped by Cambridge University to attend a concert by a musician called Edmund Delaval. Edmund was a wine glass player. He arranged wine glasses on a table. Each glass was filled with different quantity of water and he played them by rubbing their rims. Since the wine glasses were filled with different quantities of water, they produced different notes when their rims were rubbed with wet finger.

Benjamin enjoyed the ethereal music but went from the concert determined to improve the musical instruments he just heard. Arranging wine glasses with various amounts of water was not the most convenient musical instrument after all. The musician had to arrange them just so every time.

He worked with a glassblower in England for over two years and came up with an instrument he called armonica. He arranged a set of glass bowls, each different in size and thickness of the glass, held together by a rotating shaft. By spinning the shaft with a foot pedal, and running a wet finger over the rims of the glass bowl, the instrument produced magical music. "Of all my inventions," Benjamin said, "the glass armonica has given me the greatest personal satisfaction."

Soon, Benjamin's armonica became a sensation in Europe. Mozart and Beethoven composed music for armonica. However, by 1820s, a rumor spread that armonica could make people insane. Its popularity went down and armonica vanished from the music scene.

Bifocal Lenses

As he reached old age, Benjamin developed both near- and far-sightedness. His eyes could not see objects neither near or far. This meant he had to use two glasses depending on what he was looking at: outside, he needed long distance lenses, but when he had to examine something up close, he had to change glasses. Benjamin found this extremely frustrating. To solve this problem, he simply cut both the glasses in half and joined two halves from each lens together in one frame giving him the bifocal lenses.

Aside from a few changes and improvements, bifocal lenses have remained unchanged to this day. Even in his day, there were different lenses for near- and far-sightedness but it took Benjamin to put them together in one frame.

The Lightning Rod

Lightning was a menace to cities throughout the world where buildings were made mostly of wood. A direct lightning strike destroyed the house and sometimes even the entire neighborhood completely. Churches were especially vulnerable to lightning strikes. In Benjamin's time, a bolt of lightning even killed 3000 people in Italy after it struck a church basement packed with gunpowder.

In 1748, at the age of 42, Benjamin retired as a publisher. He had built enough fortune to see him through his life. Now he shifted his attention to scientific experiments, and his first experiment was with static electricity. After countless hours of tinkering, he figured that if a metal rod can be fixed on the top of the building and wired to the ground, the lightning will pass into the ground. His invention saved countless homes throughout the world. Today's lightning rod is, again, essentially the same as the one Benjamin used for his house.

Urinary Catheter

Benjamin's invention even extended to the medical world. His elder brother John suffered from kidney stones and the remedy was to insert rigid metal tubes into the urethra to drain urine every day. It was an excruciatingly painful procedure due to the rigidity of the metal tubes. Benjamin worked with a local silversmith to create catheter with hinged tubes which was flexible. He mailed it off to his brother with instructions on how to use it.

Electricity Experiments

Benjamin did not discover electricity, as is most commonly believed. That discovery came many decades before Benjamin was born. But he made significant contribution to this field. With his famous kite experiment, he showed that lightning and electricity were made of the same stuff. He was the first one to propose that electricity had fluid property, that it was able to pass from one body to the next. He also demonstrated the positive and negative charges. To share his discoveries, Benjamin invented many terms such as battery, charges, plus (positive), minus (negative), conductor, condenser and electric fire (electricity). His writings on electricity made him an American celebrity in Europe where he received multiple honors.

These are but some of Benjamin's scientific inventions. He is also credited with the discovery of Gulf Stream, a fast-moving current of warm water that runs between the US and continental Europe. He is credited with creating the first political cartoon calling for unity of the colonies against threats from other countries. In his old age, he built a mechanical arm, similar to the garbage picker of today, to reach books in his library.

Only one thing matched his ingenious inventions. He never took out patent on any of his inventions. If he did, he would have amassed fortune. He believed that his inventions should be for the good of everyone and that ideas should be shared freely.

IX: The Founding Father

As a country, the United States of America started its roots as English colonies. In 1600s and 1700s, English colonists, backed by the crown of England, started arriving in the eastern shores of the United States. The early colonists cleared forests and set up villages which became towns. Early settlers came mostly from England but there were also Germans and other Europeans looking for better lives away from their homeland. Benjamin Franklin's father was one of the early settlers to flee England and settle in Boston.

Pennsylvania, whose capital city is Philadelphia, was also a colony. In 1681, the King of England gave the province of Pennsylvania to a person called William Penn to settle a debt. At that time in Europe, people were imprisoned and punished if they had different religious beliefs. After all, it was the time when people were burnt at stake as witches. William Penn wanted Pennsylvania to be a place for religious freedom. This proved to be a big attraction for English and other Europeans who wanted better lives, free from persecution.

With the vast, open land of the new world, and the hard work of the early colonists, the colonies grew and prospered. By 1775, there were a total of 13 English colonies with around two and half million settlers.

The English colonies were the property of the British Empire. But the colonies were also given great freedom to make their own rules. They were given a high degree of autonomy and self-governance.

Gradually, however, the British crown began to exert

greater control over the colonies. After all, with the colonies prospering, it was a good source of income for the crown in the form of taxes. One of the earliest taxes Britain introduced on the colonies was the Stamp Act of 1765 which was passed by the British parliament. This act required legal documents and printed materials in the colonies to be stamped and taxed.

This tax did not go down well the colonists. The main reason was that American colonies did not have representatives in the British parliament. They were taxed without representation.

The Stamp Act was eventually removed. But the British parliament introduced more taxes for the colonies. One such tax was on tea. Tea was a popular beverage in Britain and in the colonies. To help the tea companies make more revenue, the British parliament enacted the Tea Act, that levied taxes on tea sold to the colonies. Even though the tax was not high, the colonies were angry at the effort of the British parliament to bring the colonies under British control.

In November 1773, an English ship carrying tea docked in Boston harbor. Angry colonists tried to send the ship and the tea back to England but Governor Hutchinson of

A depiction of Boston Tea Party

Massachusetts, who had business interests in the tea import, refused to send the tea back. On the night of 16 December 1773, a group of protesters, some dressed as native American warriors, boarded the ship carrying the tea and threw all of it into the water. This event came to be known as the Boston Tea Party. It was the beginning of the American War of Independence.

The British government was infuriated by the Boston

event. The British navy put a blockade of the Boston harbor and tried to restore British authority in Massachusetts. Benjamin Franklin, whose home town was Boston, offered to pay the British for the loss they incurred in Boston, but this was rejected by the British government.

While the harsh reaction of the British government was meant to put the colonies in line, this had an opposite effect. Rather than subduing the colonies, the British government's reaction further united the colonies. The First Continental Congress, a meeting of representatives from all thirteen, except one, colonies took place in Philadelphia in September 1774. The colonies put up a joint demand to the king of England to withdraw their coercive actions against the colonies. This was not accepted by Britain and fighting between American revolutionaries and British forces started in April 1775.

In May 1775, the Second Continental Congress made up of delegates from all thirteen colonies met again in Philadelphia. Benjamin Franklin was a delegate from Philadelphia. The Second Continental Congress functioned as the first national government of the United States throughout the American War of Independence. The Congress appointed committee of five to draft the Declaration of Independence. The five included Thomas Jefferson and Benjamin Franklin. In July 1775, the Congress adopted and signed the Declaration of Independence.

Presentation of the Declaration of Independence

In 1776, Benjamin was sent to France as an agent of the colonies, effectively the first diplomat of the United States. His main task was to get the support of France, then an enemy of Britain, for American independence.

Benjamin was welcomed in France with open arms. His inventions and scientific works on electricity has already made him a pop star in France. Even though he had difficulty with the French language at first, Benjamin's superior knowledge of human nature made him fit perfectly into the high culture of Paris among the elite and nobility. Through his charm and wit, he was able to bring the French to recognize the independence of the United States, provide a large sum of financial and military support in the fight against the British, and sign a military alliance with the young nation. This was one of the turning points in the American Revolutionary War in favor of the United States.

In 1783, Britain and the United States signed the peace treaty in Paris, ending the war and giving independence to the United States. Benjamin was one of the signatories from the new nation.

Having completed his task and the independence won, Benjamin returned to Philadelphia from Paris in 1785. He was given a hero's welcome and was elected as the president of Pennsylvania. He was reelected again in 1787, and sent as a delegate to the convention for the framing of the US constitution.

Benjamin is the only founding father who signed all the four documents: Declaration of Independence, the Alliance with France, Peace Treaty with England and the Constitution of the United States of America.

Benjamin Franklin retired from the public life in 1788 and died on April 17, 1790 in Philadelphia.

X: Wise Words of Benjamin Franklin

1.   Early to bed and early to rise, makes a man healthy, wealthy and wise.

2.   It is easier to prevent bad habit than to break them.

3.   Eat to please yourself but dress to please others.

4.   There are three faithful friends: an old wife, an

old dog, and ready money.

5.   There are three things extremely hard: steel, a diamond and to know oneself.

6.   The Sun never repents of the good it does, nor does it ever demand a recompence.

7.   The things which hurt, instruct.

8.   The way to be safe is never to be secure.

9.   Three good meals a day is bad living.

10.   A full belly is the mother of all evil.

11.   To lengthen your life, lessen your meals.

12.   Think of three things: where you came from, where you are going and to whom you must account.

13.   Well done is better than well said.

14.   All things are easy to industry, all things difficult

to sloth.

15.   At the working man's house hunger looks in but dares not enter.

16.   When you are good to others, you are best to yourself.

17.   Fear to do ill, and you need fear nothing.

18.   Fish and visitors stink in three days.

19.   Fools multiply folly.

20.   Save while you can; no morning sun lasts a whole day.

21.   Friendship cannot live with ceremony nor without civility.

22.   Generous minds are all of kin.

23.   Glass, china and reputation are easily cracked and never well mended.

24.   God gives all things to industry.

25.   A lean award is better than a fat judgment.

26.   God help them who help themselves.

27.   Great modesty often hides great merit.

28.   Great talkers, little doers.

29.   Half the truth is often a great lie.

30.   Here comes the orator, with his flood of words, and his drop of reason.

31.   He is a fool that cannot conceal his wisdom.

32.   He that can have patience can have what he will.

33.   He that cannot obey cannot command.

34.   He that falls in love with himself will have no

rivals.

35.   He that has a trade has an office of profit and honor.

36.   He that pursues two hares at once, does not catch one and lets the other go.

37.   He that resolves to mend hereafter resolves not to mend now.

38.   The worst wheel of the cart makes the most noise.

39.   He that sows thorns should never go barefoot.

40.   A false friend and a shadow attend only when sun shines.

41.   There is none deceived but he that trusts.

42.   Trust yourself and another will not betray you.

43.   He that waits upon fortune is never sure of

dinner.

44.   He that won't be counselled can't be helped.

45.   Hope of gain lessens pains.

46.   How few there are who have courage enough to own their faults.

47.   If passion drives, let reason hold the reins.

48.   If you would be beloved, make yourself amiable.

49.   There was never a good knife made of bad steel.

50.   They who have nothing to trouble them, will be troubled at nothing.

51.   A flatterer never seems absurd: the flattered always takes his word.

52.   The same man cannot be both a friend and

flatterer.

53.   An honest man will receive neither money nor praise that is not his due.

54.   Haste makes waste.

55.   Have you somewhat to do tomorrow? Do it today.

56.   Having been poor is no shame, but being ashamed of it, is.

57.   Hear no ill of a friend, nor speak any of an enemy.

58.   Don't judge of men's wealth or piety by their Sunday appearances.

59.   Don't throw stones at your neighbors if your own windows are glass.

60.   Don't go to the doctor with every distemper, nor to the lawyer with every quarrel, nor to the pot

for every thirst.

61.   Do you love life? Then do not squander time; for that is the stuff life is made of.

62.   Drunkenness, that worst of evils, makes some men fools, some beasts, some devils.

63.   Diligence is the mother of good luck.

64.   Being ignorant is not so much a shame as being unwilling to learn.

65.   If you have time, don't wait for time.

66.   If you know how to spend less than you get, you have the philosopher's stone.

67.   If your riches are yours, why don't you take them with you to the other world.

68.   If you would be loved, love and be loveable.

69.   It is better to take many injuries, than to give

one.

70.   It is the easiest thing in the world for a man to deceive himself.

71.   If you would not be forgotten as soon as you are dead and rotten, either write things worth reading, or do things worth writing.

72.   Lend money to an enemy and you will gain him; to a friend and you will lose him.

73.   Love your enemies for they tell you your faults.

74.   Let every new year find you a better man.

75.   Little strokes fell great oaks.

76.   Lost time is never found again.

77.   The sleeping fox catches no poultry.

78.   The second vice is lying. The first is running in debt.

79.   Many dishes, many diseases.

80.   Meanness is the mother of insolence.

81.   Men and melons are hard to know.

82.   Men take more pains to mask then mend.

83.   No gains without pains.

84.   Nothing but money is sweeter than honey.

85.   A light purse is a heavy curse.

86.   Beware of little expenses. A small leak will sink
a great ship.

87.   An empty bag cannot stand upright.

88.   Nothing dries sooner than a tear.

89.   Now I have a sheep and a cow, everybody bids

me good morrow.

90.   Observe all men; yourself the most.

91.   Pay what you owe and you will know what's your own.

92.   Poverty, poetry and new titles of honor make men ridiculous.

93.   Praise to the undeserving is severe satire.

94.   Presumption first blinds a man, then sets him a running.

95.   Pride dines upon vanity, sups on contempt.

96.   The proud hates pride – in others.

97.   Reading makes a full man, meditation a profound man, discourse a clear man.

98.   Search other for their virtues, yourself for vices.

99.   Be at war with your vices, at peace with your neighbors.

100. Since you are not sure of a minute, don't throw away an hour.

101. Time enough always proves little enough.

102. The bird that sits is easily shot.

103. The cat in gloves catches no mice.

104. Speak little, do much.

105. Success has ruined many a man.

106. The doors of wisdom are never shut.

107. The eye of a master will do more work than hand.

108. The honey is sweet but the bee has a sting.

109. The most exquisite folly is made of wisdom

spun too fine.

110. The noblest question in the world is what good may I do in it?

111. The poor have little, beggars none, the rich too much, enough not one.

112. Fear not death; for the sooner we die, the longer shall we be immortal.

113. Death takes no bribes.

114. Take courage, mortal. Death can't banish you out of the universe.

115. Wish not so much to live long as to live well.

www.ingramcontent.com/pod-product-compliance
Lightning Source LLC
Chambersburg PA
CBHW051241160726
47994CB00002B/969